JAKE

AN AUTOBIOGRAPHY OF A DYNAMIC DOG

Interpreted by: Fred Coats

A Note to Readers:

My name is Jake, my human sister called me Jakearooni, and I lived an extraordinary life. From the time I was a pup, meeting my family for the first time, to an older dog my personality and antics had my humans laughing, crying, and sometime even nodding knowingly at my wisdom. You see, I was very animated so everyone knew exactly what I was thinking. If you've ever wondered what your dog is thinking, I might be able to shed some light on that.

Enjoy!

Table of Contents

About the Author

Fred was born in Milwaukee, Wisconsin. He spent the majority of his career working in the Milwaukee area.

He retired to Knoxville, Tennessee with his wife after spending his last 10 years working in Birmingham, Alabama.

They now enjoys hiking the Smoky Mountains and Fred enjoys a hobby of routing wooden signs. He smiles each time he comes upstairs from his shop when he sees the painting of JAKE on the wall.

JAKE

Introduction

This is a true-life story of a wonderful dog that shared many great years of happiness with us. As all dogs do, he was always there with a tail wagging to greet you. No matter what kind of day you may have had, it was always better the minute you saw Jake.

We had wonderful dogs prior to Jake and for about two years we went without a dog. We figured with the kids grown and gone, that maybe we wouldn't get another. It is amazing how things turn out. One day at work, some of my co-workers were talking about dogs and I mentioned that I couldn't believe that my wife had never asked to get another dog. Well, at supper that very evening she mentioned, out of the blue, that maybe we should look for another dog.

From the very start, we knew that we wanted to get a dog from the Humane Society. So whenever my wife went by the area, she would stop and look to see if that "special" dog was there. There were many trips in the weeks following that supper conversation, but still the right dog wasn't there.

On a Saturday, my daughter Cindy and I were going shopping and would pass near the Humane Society. My wife instructed me to stop and look. Low and behold, there was a whole litter of pups! I felt one of them would definitely fill our needs. I picked out a little female and my daughter agreed. We called home and told my wife to get there right away, because we thought we had found the dog for her. When she arrived I held up that cute little female. She took one look, picked up a little male and said, "Nope. This is the one...and his name is Jake."

It was agreed that we would adopt the male, and indeed he would be named Jake. Then we had to wait for 24 hours.

The Humane Society requires a waiting period to be sure people do not change their minds. Well, we knew we weren't going to do that, so we would have another dog the following day.

This book is Jake's story, or as his sister nicknamed him, Jake-a-rooni. From here on we will let Jake tell you his tale.

My First Year

Life at the Humane Society

Hi. My name is Jake, but sometimes I am also called Jake-a-rooni. I like both, so you can call me by either name. I want to tell you the story of my wonderful life and how I had what any dog could possibly wish for.

I was born in Wisconsin and I had a bunch of sisters and brothers. (I was young then so I hadn't learned how to count yet). We all ended up at the Humane Society in Waukesha, Wisconsin. I was kept in a large kennel with my brothers and sisters. Boy, can you just imagine how hard it is to take a nap with all those other dogs climbing all over you? I guess I can't complain too much because I remember climbing on top of them when they were sleeping also.

Even though it was crowded, the nighttime was so lonely that it was nice to have my brother and sisters with me. Even with all the other dogs in the Humane Society, it was really quiet and a little scary for us young pups at night. We missed our Mom and so we all cuddled up together and slept. During the daytime it was pretty busy. People would come and go, and some people would pick some of us up and remark how cute we were. Then one day, my Dad and human sister came—only I didn't know they would be my Dad and sister at that time. My Dad picked up one of my sisters. They talked to her kind of funny and said how cute she was. Then I heard them call my "to be" Mom and told her to come and take a look. I felt so lonely, I just wished it had been me they were looking at. They stayed and played with all of us until my new Mom arrived. When my Dad picked up my sister and asked how she liked her, she said "No." Then she picked me up and said "This is the one, and his name is Jake." You can never imagine how hard my heart was beating…I was so happy. I had to be very careful not to wet on her, as I was THAT excited. I kind of felt sorry for my sister, but not too sorry.

I had already heard about the rule the Humane Society had

about making humans wait 24 hours before they could take a dog home. This was to be sure they really wanted a pet. Let me tell you, for the next 24 hours, my heart was beating so fast. Every time I saw the door open, I was hoping it would be them. After what seemed like way more than one day, the door opened, and in walked my new Mom and my new sister. I was so excited I was running around, jumping on top of all of my brothers and sisters. I was giving them all goodbye kisses before I left them.

The people at the Waukesha Wisconsin Humane Society took really good care of me and my family. As the time came for me to leave, I think they were as happy for me as my new Mom and sister were. They gave me big hugs and rubs before I left.

The First Few Days

You can't begin to know how excited I was to start my new life. I was a really excited puppy riding in my sister's lap, while my Mom drove the car. Little did I know what I had to look forward to when we got to my new home.

As the car pulled into the driveway, kids appeared from everywhere. At first I thought…Wow! Are these all in my family? Then I found out that they weren't all family, but rather all the kids in the neighborhood. They knew I was coming and they couldn't wait to see me. My new Dad was also there with them waiting to see me again.

When my sister got me out of the car and put me down, all the kids went wild. They all wanted to pet me, pick me up, and run

around with me. I never realized that I would have so much fun so soon. When the kids did pick me up, they were told to be careful and not hurt me. Heck, I didn't care…I was happy. I gave them all a big kiss when they picked me up. We played and played and spent a lot of time running around.

When I saw my new backyard, I thought that it was so big that I would never be able to run from one end to the other. As

the kids chased me, I romped around having the best time of my young life. My Dad, Mom, and sister kept a close eye that nobody would be too rough with me, but I was having a ball. With all this excitement I didn't realize that there were some other "new" family members there. I found out that my Dad's brother, his wife, and son were visiting from Florida (wherever that is). They told me they were my new uncle, aunt and cousin. So much to learn for such a young puppy, but I was determined to remember who everyone was. My cousin really liked me and I liked him.

Later, when the kids left and we went into the house I was so tired that I took a short nap before I even got a chance to look around my new house. As a young puppy, I wasn't used to all of this excitement.

After a nap I was able to explore a little. It seemed it was okay for me to go wherever I wanted. There was a large family room that was down a step, so when I first went in there I kind of fell on my face. Everyone was ready to come to my rescue but heck, I was okay. I did need to get a little boost from Mom going back up the step, because that was kind of hard.

I had my own little area in the laundry room with both a water and food dish. I drank a lot of water, as I had had a busy day. I did a pretty good job of chowing down my dinner too. We then spent a few hours in the family room just visiting.

I was trying to learn all I could because I wanted to make sure they all loved me as much as I was loving them and my new home. When it came to bedtime, my Mom and Dad put me in a cage right next to the bed. It had some nice soft blankets and a towel and some toys. I cried a little as I laid there, because I was a little lonesome for my brother and sisters. When you are used to sleeping in a pile of puppies, sleeping alone is hard. Mom reached down and put her fingers in my cage and touched me. She talked gently to me until I went to sleep and slept well all night.

In the morning when I woke up, I *really* had to go potty. I didn't want to go in my cage and mess up my really soft bed. I made a few cries and my Mom got up, let me out of the cage, and took me right outside. It didn't take me long to do what I had to do. I was still so excited that as soon as I was done, I ran back to my Mom with my heart pumping a mile a minute. I was realizing that I was a very lucky dog.

I enjoyed this quiet time with my Mom, not knowing that this was just the beginning of a very busy day for me. Later on, a lot more people came to our house. They came to see my Uncle Bill, Aunt Kathy and Cousin Sean from Florida. Another brother of my Dad, Uncle Bob and his wife Aunt Cathy, came and brought their dog. At first I didn't like the idea of another dog in my house, but I learned that he would be leaving when Uncle Bob and Aunt Cathy left, so I felt better about him. Then, some of my Dad's cousins came. Their names were Eddie and Mindy. Needless to say, I had another very busy day meeting lots of new people.

And then it got EVEN busier. My "new" brother Kevin came over with his wife and their kids, Danny and Bryan. I was getting so much attention and being held so much that I was beginning to think that I might not ever have to walk again. Either way, I wasn't about to complain. After another exciting day I was really ready to go to bed when the time came. I cried a little because I knew if I did, Mom would touch me and talk to me. I was right! I am so happy and lucky that I was the dog that they picked! I sighed softly and quickly went off to zonkersville.

Once again, in the morning, I was ready to go out as soon as I got up. I cried a little and once again Mom let me out of my cage and outside for me to go potty. Although I am still young, I am a quick learner. I know I wouldn't want to go in my cage, and I am so happy with my new home, so I will not go in the house. If my humans are going to take good care of me, then I am going to do whatever I can to take care of them. I want this love to keep on coming. I know that they love me and I want to tell you, I love them too.

The Next Few Weeks

All the activity slowed down the next few days. All our company left, my Dad and sister went to work, so I was home alone

all day with Mom. It was still pretty nice. While I still got a lot of attention from Mom, I could also nap whenever I wanted. One time, Mom even took a nap, so I ran to lay down in my cage to be near her. After work, Dad and Cindy came home and I started to learn what a "normal" day would be like. I am certain I am really going to like this life.

Oh, did I tell you about my Dad and his camera? Well, he sure does take a lot of pictures of me. Mom told me to expect this, as he takes pictures all the time.

One day, I was just resting on the floor when he put a can by my side. He said something about wanting to have something to compare me to when I get big. I didn't understand what he was talking about, but I guessed I would find out with time. I heard Mom and Dad talking with Cindy about taking me on my first road trip.

Their good friends, Scott and Linda, were moving to Indianapolis from out East. I was excited about going on a long car ride. Maybe all the excitement of the past week or the upcoming trip started to get to me. I wasn't

feeling too well. Mom and Dad knew I wasn't feeling good, since they didn't see me running around like normal.

Our trip was planned to go to Indianapolis but Mom told Dad they needed to take me to the vet. *Wow!* I heard about vets while I was in the Humane Society and from what I heard I didn't want anything to do with them. I didn't have any choice in this matter, though. They took me to the vet that used to take care of their other dogs. It was about 5 miles away in North Prairie, Wisconsin. When we got there, I was really afraid. Then the vet came out and she was *soooooo* nice. She picked me up, hugged me and kissed me. I started to feel better. The vet was told about our trip we were all packed for. She told my Mom and Dad that she wanted to keep an eye on me for a few hours because there is a sickness that some puppies get that can be fatal. She said she would call Mom and Dad when she finished her test. You can bet that as a young puppy, this had me a little afraid.

The next few hours were the longest hours of my young life. I was once again around other dogs but this time I wasn't feeling so good. This vet took such good care of me during my visit, but I still missed my Mom and Dad. I wanted them to come and get me. After a few hours, I heard the vet call my Mom and Dad and say that I would be okay. I just needed some medicine and they could come and get me. You want to know who was a happy dog? Well, that was me!

After picking me up, we started our road trip (my *first* road trip) to Indianapolis. Mom told me to get used to it, because I would be making a lot of road trips with them. I figured this is fine with me as long as I'm with them. I was in the back seat with Cindy and she was giving me all the attention I wanted. I even took a few short naps with my head on her lap.

We spent the weekend with Scott and Linda, but they had failed to mention the other "dogs." Their names were Yankee and Brewer and they were really big! They were, however, pretty nice. Yankee seemed a little older and he wasn't too interested in me. I'm also not so sure they were all that happy having a young dog around. They were really lucky I still wasn't feeling 100% or I would have given them a run for their money. I was feeling better each day, but by the time I was ready to really run they had become accustomed to me.

On our trip home, I decided that riding in the car was pretty nice. I shared the whole back seat with Cindy again, so I could look out the window, or lie down, or put on some of my puppy charm and Cindy would hold me in her lap. Sometimes Cindy would let Mom hold me in her lap in the front seat. (I'm starting to figure out these humans, and I really like them.)

Puppy School

Mom and Dad signed me up to go to puppy school at the same vet that had taken care of me when I was sick. I knew this would be okay because the vet was so nice to me when I wasn't feeling good. My only concern is wondering what I could learn at school. I think for a young guy that I am learning pretty darn fast. I figured, what the heck; let's give it a try.

I found out that this class would last about 4 weeks (bear with me, the one thing I haven't learned yet is to count). There were other dogs there with their owners. I'm glad my Mom and Dad were with me. The start of class each week was a lot of fun. All of us puppies got to play together. We would jump on each other, and bark, and just have a ball. It kind of reminded me of when I was in the kennel with my brothers and sisters at the Humane Society.

Each week at school, we had playtime, but then we had to study—I guess that's what schools are all about. I won't go into a lot of detail here, but we did learn a lot of stuff in all of the classes. We learned to sit, shake hands, and we were shown how to "stay." We also learned how to listen to our owners.

There were a couple of classes that were kind of scary. In one class they had a small slide and we had to learn how to slide down this slide. I wonder what I will ever need this information for in the future? In another class we had to crawl through a long tunnel. It was kind of scary, but I heard my Mom and Dad calling me at the other end, so I felt safe. I must admit, I did run through it pretty fast, because I wanted to get in and out as quickly as possible.

After the classes were finished, we graduated. We had a little party with cookies and got to play together, for the last time. The vet told all the Moms and Dads that the next thing we all needed to do was spend a lot of time around other people, kids, and dogs.

She also said we should be taken for rides in the car. She told them it was very important for us puppies to learn how to "socialize." I know I can do that because I love people and attention, and I really like riding in the car.

A Puppy Having Fun

Once I became an "educated puppy" (remember earlier when I told you I thought I was pretty smart....well, I was just getting smarter by the day) it was time for me to have some plain old puppy fun. Our routine had settled in, so I pretty much knew what to expect each day. I got up in the morning, went potty, then played. Then I played some more and explored my yard. Oh, and don't forget, Mom and I always had to have our daily nap. She may not have needed one, but boy I sure did with all that activity. Then, when we got up, it was playtime some more.

I was also busy learning other new things. Each day we went for a long walk. Mom and Dad said it was exercise that they needed. I got a lot more exercise than they did because I was still small and I had to take a lot more steps for each one of theirs. A lot of the time our neighbors across the street, Dave and Sue, walked with us. Sometimes my Mom had to drag Dave out, because he did not want to walk. He started work in the middle of the night so he was tired when we walked. Mom didn't take that as an excuse and made him come along. When we walked, Mom and Dad made me keep a leash on. They didn't want me to run away (Like with the life I had, why would I have wanted to do that??)

Remember when I told you how smart I was? Well, I kept getting smarter by the day. I had a problem when we walked. If I got too far out on my leash I would get tangled up when we went past a mailbox. Then Mom would have to walk me around the right way. It didn't take me long to learn that when I came up to one of those mailbox poles, I should have gone back near the road so I wouldn't get tangled up. I was so smart!

Well, I found out that maybe I had not completed all of my "smart" training. I was beginning to feel like I had everything under control, including Mom and Dad. We were inside playing and having a good time. We had two sofas and I would run and jump from one to the other. Mom and Dad weren't too impressed with that. They put some pennies in a coke can and as soon as I jumped on a couch they would throw a can without me knowing it. Boy, that would really scare me!! It didn't take too many times before I figured the floor would be just fine with me. I figured I had done pretty well up to that point; since that was the first time I had to be disciplined.

Earlier, I told you about Dad and all the pictures. Well, I was beginning to wonder what he really looked like. He always seemed to have that camera in his face, taking pictures of me. He didn't realize that I really knew what he was doing (but I wasn't going to tell him). This actually helped me learn a very important word. That word was *"COOKIE."* If I saw Dad with his camera and if I didn't pay attention to him, he would say something like "Jake, I have a cookie for you." I would immediately pose for his picture and he would give me a cookie. With all the pictures he took, I found that I really liked that word.

During the day when it was just Mom and I, we would spend a lot of time outside. Mom liked to work in her yard and I loved playing out there. Being as small as I was, I could go into the shrubbery and pretend I was in the forest. If I saw a little bug I would jump after him. I was not too fast then and I was still a little clumsy. Mom and Dad had a swimming pool but it was way, way too big for me. I pretended my water dish was my swimming pool and splashed around in it. I was pretty careful because I didn't want to get all my beautiful hair wet.

Road Trip #2

It wasn't long before it was time for my second road trip. Mom and Dad said we were going to see "Grandma." This was Mom's mother and she lived in Hayward, which was way up north in Wisconsin. On this trip I had the whole back seat to myself, since Cindy had to stay at home and go to work. Car riding was a pretty good deal; I could relax and rest my young bones.

Once again, Mom and Dad had failed to tell me about another dog. This one was Grandma's and her name was Buttons. She really wasn't impressed with me being there. I kept trying to play but she would just snap at me. By now you can probably guess what my Dad did. Yup, he took a picture of me and Buttons because we were about the same size. He said it would be neat to look back at it when  I got bigger. I thought Dad was taking this comparison thing a little too far, don't you? But hey, what can I say, I got another cookie.

Grandma lived on a lake and boy was it ever big! I thought Mom and Dad's pool was big but that lake...I couldn't even see across it. Even though it was really big, it was a little better for me because it wasn't very deep when you first got in. I found I could walk in and just get my legs wet. One more thing about this lake, it was really cold. I could have drunk this water because it was colder than what was in my dish. I heard Mom talk about swimming in this lake. I sure wouldn't do that, it would be way too cold for me.

Grandma also had a great big area with a lot of trees. I really had fun playing and exploring in the woods. I did need to be careful though, as there were some trees that had fallen over and I got caught up in some of the branches once. It was also hard for me to jump over some of the trunks of the trees with my little legs. Then, guess what I found? Squirrels…boy are they ever fun to chase! Only problem was, if you got too close, they would run up a tree, which wasn't fair because they knew I couldn't climb trees (yet). Those squirrels really knew how to tease a pup. They would jump from one tree, to another, to another, and then come down and let you chase them some more.

By the time I was done playing with these squirrels, I was ready for a nap. One cool thing was that Buttons had a great big pillow that she slept on. I heard Mom call it a beanbag chair. It sure was fun to crawl into and move around. I was having so much fun with it, I heard Mom tell Grandma that she was going to make me one. She said they used to have one for the other dogs and she would just have to re-cover it. I could hardly wait!

With all the activity up North, the ride home went really fast. I think I was asleep as soon as we got out of the driveway. I really stretched out in the back seat. After a quick gas stop in Eau Claire, it was on to home and back to a more normal life.

A Normal Life

Now that we were back home, I could concentrate on learning more and work on growing up. Apparently I was going to get bigger because Dad kept taking pictures of me to compare in the future. I still got to romp around the yard and had put to good use some of the tricks I learned while I was in the woods by Grandma. I could really chase all kinds of critters.

One thing I never could figure out was Dad kept trying to have me chase this plastic toy called a Frisbee. He told me that a dog they had before me named Cha-Sam was a State champion in the Frisbee competition. He would throw that thing and apparently I was supposed to run after it and catch it in my mouth. Then I was supposed to bring it back so he could throw it again. I am sorry, but I could never get into that game very well. I wondered how he would like to run around with a fur coat in the summer and catch a Frisbee in his mouth? I had to give Dad credit; he sure did work hard at trying to get me to do this. I did however learn a new game for myself while Dad tried to get me to catch the Frisbee. I noticed that if it was sunny, I could see the shadow of the Frisbee on the ground. I started having more fun chasing the shadow than I did the Frisbee. Poor Dad. He finally decided that I wouldn't be the next Frisbee champion in the family. But wow, did I ever have fun with my new game and I didn't even need any of the family members to help me play it. I saw a bird fly over and noticed it had a shadow...and man, I took off after it. Then, another bird, then another. I was having a blast. My Dad thought as long as I liked this game so much he would play it in the house with me. He would shine a flashlight and I would chase the light on the floor. I felt better knowing Dad had a game he could play with me.

Mom and Dad continued to take me to places where there were a lot of people and other dogs, so that I got used to being around them. I liked this because I loved to be outside and I really loved it when people would come up and pet me and remark what a cute puppy I was. We went to an exhibition the fire department put on. There were a lot of adults, kids and dogs. This one dog looked sort of funny, he had a fire helmet on and had a face that sort of looked like a dog and a human. He walked on just his two hind legs and was able to pick me up with his other two. They said he was a fire dog but I couldn't figure him out at all.

It made me happy when Danny and Bryan came over. I liked to have them play with me. Another thing I really liked (but don't tell anyone) was being able to take some of Bryan's food right out of his hand. I thought Bryan liked to do this but I had to be careful, because Danny would tell Grandma that Bryan was feeding me, then she would yell at me not to take that food. Then Mom found an answer to that prob-lem. We had a playpen for Bryan. I thought maybe they would put Bryan in there but I was so wrong. I was the one that got put in the play-pen, while Bryan ate his snacks. Not fair! This

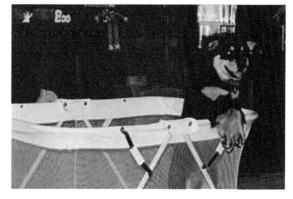

got me on the trail of liking human food instead of puppy food. I would have to see what I could do about getting some more of that.

One day, Mom was getting the dishwasher ready to wash the dishes and when she left the room for a minute, I jumped up and  started licking...*yum-yum!* Oh yea, guess what, I got yelled at again. Trust me, I had not given up on the human food thing. I was going to have to sit down and figure out what I could do to get some more. Heck, if I had my way, I would be able to write a whole book on that subject, because it tasted *sooooo* good.

I found out about a really special day that everyone has, it's called a "Birthday." This is the day of the year you were born. Every year on this day people throw a party for you. Dad had a birthday on the 7th of August and Mom on the 19th of August. Some of the neighbors and cousins came over, and of course Danny and Bryan came. On each occasion they had some food and then they had cake. Once again, I was able to work with my little buddy Bryan and eat some out of his hands. I had to be careful though, so Mom and Dad didn't see me do this, or I might get yelled at again. Man…was that stuff ever good. Then, Danny had his Birthday on August 20th, one day after Mom's. Not only did he get cake AND food, but he got lots of toys too. That was a really fun day. I asked Mom why her and Dad didn't get a lot of stuff and she said they didn't get much for each other on birthdays because if they needed something they could just get it when they needed it. This birthday thing really got me thinking. I asked Mom when my birthday was. She said that they weren't exactly sure of the exact date but it was close to July 4th so that's the day they claimed for my birthday. She explained all about Independence Day and then I felt really proud to have a birthday on that date. I asked when Bryan's was and she said not until November.

Summer Turns to Fall and Winter

With the cooler weather coming I found it much nicer to be outside more. I could run around and play and not get so hot. I also found out that I was getting bigger. Actually, I found this out because good old Dad got out the coke can and the camera. Yup, I was getting a lot bigger. Heck, someday I may even be able to hold a coke can in my mouth.

Then, I had another new experience. Mom called it Halloween. Man, you should have seen this place. There were all kinds of spooky things all around the house. Mom even made a scary creature that she put near the fireplace.

At first I was scared of it, but then I noticed it never moved so I figured I was ok with it. Mom explained how kids go door to door and get candy from the people when they were dressed up funny. I started to figure; could it be a possibility of human food? If so, I needed to learn quickly. Mom said no, it was just candy and dogs can't have candy. That was a bummer, but boy, did I ever have fun when kids came to the

door! Of course, with me still being a puppy, they all wanted to pet me. I liked that petting thing. It felt so good, why, I would have to say that it would be second to eating human food.

At any rate, I enjoyed all the kids with their crazy costumes, even though I didn't recognize some of my very own neighbor kids when they were dressed up. I

heard them say "Hi Jake" and wondered how they knew my name. Mom even made me my own costume. She called it a bandana and put it around my neck. I must say, I looked pretty good in it. It was a fun day, but then again every day was a fun day for me.

Next thing I knew, we were having a party for Bryan because it was his birthday. It must have been November. I figured I could get lots of that good party food from him, because he always shared it with me. Besides, if he set food down to play with one of his new toys, man, I would get the food... *yum!* I still had to be very careful so Mom and Dad didn't see me or I might have had to go into Bryan's play pen again.

I learned November brought another party time called Thanksgiving. The big deal about this day was food...and as you know by now, *I WAS INTO FOOD!* I couldn't believe how good the house smelled all day long. I was right alongside Mom all day because if any food fell off the counter, I didn't want her to have to bend down to pick it up. So, I worked extra hard watching for anything to drop. Did I mention to you that I love human food? I liked human food so much that I started to beg at the table and they told me I had to lay down when they ate. Again, *NOT FAIR!* Well, I must have done a very good job helping mom all day, because after they had their dinner they gave me some samples in my dog bowl. Thanksgiving was the *BEST* day!

It wasn't too long after this Thanksgiving feast that I experienced my first snow. Boy, was that stuff ever cold! It was fun to run around in and I even got to make my first snowball. Mom and Dad told me to wait, there would be plenty more of that com-

ing. Sure enough, one night we got a lot of snow, why it was almost too deep for me to walk in. Cindy put on a hat she called a "Santa Hat" and put a bandana on me and had Dad take a picture of us. Cindy said she was going to use this on her Christmas cards. I didn't know what she was talking about, but I was soon to find out.

Christmas. Man oh man—this had to be the greatest thing ever. Now, you should have seen our house. It was all decorated again. This time there were lights everywhere and the entire house was decorated really, really nice. I thought this was going to be my favorite holiday. Do you want to know why? Food! Mom made cookies, cookies, and more cookies...and then *MORE* cookies. These are human cookies I'm talking about, not the doggie kind Dad gave me when he took my picture. Let me tell you, there was no doubt which one I would take if I had a choice. Whenever Mom was making cookies, I did my super job of making sure to clean up *ANYTHING* that should fall on the floor. Once in a while she would give me a little taste of raw cookie dough and that stuff was good even before it was baked. Then Mom said I was doing a very good job in helping fight Global Warming. She gave me all of the bowls to lick out when she was finished with them. She said that way she didn't have to use hot water to rinse them out, which is bad for Global Warming. I wanted to tell you, knowing this new bit of information, I did an extra special job on every bowl that came my way. Mom made so many different kinds of cookies and so many of each kind, I kept wondering how they were going to eat them all. I assure you, I would be willing to do whatever I needed to do to help them get rid of them…yum! But again, Mom said no, she gave out tins of cookies as gifts. I wondered if there was a tin marked for "Jake-a-rooni?"

After the cookies were all baked and put away, Mom and Dad did still more decorating. Can you believe that Mom and Dad actually cut down a tree and put it up in the family room? I am seeing new things every day. Then they put all kinds of lights and ornaments all over that tree. I must admit, I didn't understand some of this human stuff, but the tree did look pretty neat. The next thing you know, Mom was busy wrapping presents and putting them under the tree. She did tell me that there were some presents for me, but I had to wait until Christmas to open them.

When Christmas came, we ended up with a whole house full of company. Then, when they started opening presents, we had wrapping paper all over the place. I was having fun just romping in the paper. It wasn't my favorite thing because that was still begging for small bites of cookies and food. My favorite little food buddy Bryan really came through for me. I told him to try and sneak me food so that nobody would notice me eating. That way I could get some goodies from some of the others too. Then I went around to everyone and I was given a little taste of so many good things. Dad's cousin Bev was the only really tough one on my list.

When I would go by her she always said "Forget it dog." I guess she didn't realize I was part human (the eating part). I was definitely going to have to work on softening her up some. Mom also had me working on learning something new when I did beg. She didn't like me to drool, so if it looked like I was about to beg, she would say: "Jake, don't drool." Then she would lick her lips to show me what to do. I was determined to learn how to do that because there was no way that I ever wanted to be shut off from my begging.

After the holidays were over, our house once again went back to normal. Mom said that she kept the decorations up until the end of January because she loved them so much and I agreed. Some days it was really peaceful with just Mom and I home alone.

Even though the weather outside was really getting cold, we still went for a walk each day. Dad said he would rather walk in really cold weather than to exercise on the Nordic Trac for a half hour. We generally went the same way each day and Dave and Sue went along (that is, whenever we could get Dave to go). I really liked to walk when it was snowing outside, because I could taste the snow on my tongue. If I got thirsty, I just grabbed a little mouthful of snow. (I always made sure it was clean snow.) Speaking of clean snow, each time we went on a walk, Dad took along a couple of plastic bags. That way if I did a job in someone's yard, he would pick it up and take it home. He didn't like me to leave my surprises for the people that lived along our walk.

As I continued to grow up, I still slept in my cage. The only thing that had changed was Mom and Dad had started to leave the door open so I could get out if I wanted to. It was pretty comfortable in there and besides that, I felt safe. After they saw that I was not doing anything during the night, I think they decided to test me. They were going somewhere and it would be too cold for me in the car. They left me home alone but this time they just left me out of my cage altogether. As soon as the car pulled out of the driveway, into my cage I went. I didn't want to say that I was afraid, but I sure did feel better when I was in my cage. I guess it goes back to when I was really small and Mom would put her fingers through the cage and touch me at night. When I heard the garage door open, I made a beeline for the back door, and waited for them to come in. I was so happy to see them!

Spring of My First Year

It seemed like it stayed cold for a long time and there was a lot of snow to play in. Then, all of a sudden, it started to get a little warmer outside. Then the snow started to melt and Mom said that it would soon be spring and that she and I would have a lot of work to do outside.

Mom and Dad told me they were going to spring Training so I would have to be by myself all day long while Cindy went to work. I wasn't exactly crazy about this, but theytold me there was no way for me to go along. They said they went to see the Brewers practice and play each year in Arizona.They said they liked it because the weather was really nice there at that time of the year.

Not being crazy about being home alone all day, I figured this would be a great time to show Mom, Dad and Cindy how much I loved my new house. I would be a super good boy and not chew on anything, or do any jobs in the house. Besides, I knew by then that it was my house too. Each night I would be so happy to see Cindy and she was happy to see me. We would eat and then we would play and spend the evening together. At bedtime, Cindy slept in Mom and Dad's bed while they were gone, so she could be close to me in my cage. I really liked that she did that for me. Besides, since I was getting bigger I could protect her too.

It didn't seem like a week had gone by, but all of a sudden Mom and Dad were home. I'm not sure who was the most excited; me to see them or them to see me! Either way I knew everyone was happy. That night Cindy told them what a good dog I had been all week. (Remember back when I told you I would do whatever I had to in order to make everyone happy with me? Well, I think it was working!)

Pretty soon it was time for another road trip to Grandma's house in Hayward. We went to see Grandma for Easter. Even

though we had lost all of our snow at home, Grandma still had a lot. In fact, she had some big piles of snow that I had fun digging in and playing "King of the Mountain" on. It was still so cold up there that there was ice on the lake. It was pretty neat being able to walk on water like that. Dad said he didn't like to walk on ice. (I guess we all have a little chicken in us.) It was nice to see Buttons again but she still wasn't crazy about seeing me. I was getting much bigger than her—but Dad didn't even take a comparison picture to match against the first time I saw her. That seemed pretty funny to me, but I wasn't going to say anything.

After we got home, I found out we would be going on yet another road trip. This time back to Indianapolis. I was really getting into this car riding business. It gave me time to stretch out and relax. I must admit though, I did spend some time begging. You would not believe all the goodies Mom takes along on a road trip. Seemed like her and Dad started eating goodies as soon as they got out of the driveway. They did give me little samples of some of the things I could eat but then they would tell me to go lie down.

Anyway, when we got to Indianapolis, Scott and Linda had moved into a new house. The one we visited the last time was one they had just rented while they built the new one. You should have seen this house…*Wow!* It was really big. It had three floors and was on the lake. It was really beautiful.

It seemed a little different going to Scott & Linda's house. It took me a minute, but then I realized that Yankee wasn't there. Mom and Dad told me that Yankee was old and that he had died. I felt pretty bad, but then they told me about this place that dogs go to called "Rainbow Bridge." It is a very special place where old dogs become young again and can run and play and eat everything good. Trust me, I was not in any hurry to go there because I had it pretty good where I was. I did know that dogs didn't live as long as humans did so that is why they have a special place for dogs to go to wait until their owners join them, when the human's time comes to die and go to Heaven. They meet their dogs at the Rainbow Bridge and go to Heaven with them. Well, I felt better about Yankee after that and knew that someday I would join him there while I waited for my Mom and Dad.

Brewer did show me around the new house. He said he really likes it. He had several places that he could lay down and relax or look out the windows. They also had a big deck that we could go on and look at the boats going by on the lake.

There sure were a lot of boats on this lake. Scott and Linda had two boats. One was a pontoon boat and the other was a speed boat that Scott water skied behind. We went on a boat ride in the pontoon boat. It was really neat. The wind just blew in my hair and it was fun smelling all the smells. Brewer and I had fun together when our parents went away and left us home alone. We had control of the whole house and we explored. I'm not saying that we were afraid but I know we were both pretty happy that nobody came to the door. We would have had to bark at them and I'm sure we would have barked with a question mark sound.

My Second Year

My First Birthday Party

Guess what? I was finally able to have a birthday party! Mom reminded me that they weren't exactly sure which day I was born but they knew it was around the 4th of July. Then she explained to me again about what this meant. I know that Mom sure did put out a lot of American flags. I thought they were just for my birthday party. Mom said that she had told me all about Independence Day when I was smaller and what it meant to our country. She wanted to remind me of this in case I didn't remember and because it was so important to know. After hearing her explanation, I felt really proud to have my birthday on the 4th of July. Mom even made me a bandana that looked like a flag. Let me tell you, I wore this with pride.

I figured now that I was a year old, I must be pretty much full grown. Seemed like I was growing some every day for a while and then that slowed down. I was still working hard at learning everything I could, so I could be really smart.

One thing that I learned during my first year was that it doesn't take much to have a party at our house. Tell me, did you ever hear about having a birthday party for a dog? Well, I guess you don't know my Mom and Dad. Seems like there was something going on every weekend. I liked the idea of having a party for my birthday. Would you believe that even Bev was happy to see me (I know she really, really loves me but doesn't want to let on!) Of course Dan and Bryan were at my party and they shared some of their cake with me...*yum!* They found out that I was starting to run pretty fast and I could keep up with them without any trouble. I don't know who slept better the nights they visited, them or me. I know they sure could tire me out, but I loved every minute of it. Oh, I almost forgot to tell you about my birthday present. Mom made me that bean bag bed she was talking about. It was just like the one Buttons had but it was much bigger. *Wow!* Was it ever neat and really comfortable.

As I was going to sleep that night, I thought to myself that it doesn't take a birthday for Mom and Dad to have a party. Most every weekend Dave and Sue and Bev and Dale come over. If they were not here, Mom and Dad would go to one of their houses to see them. Those three couples got along really well and spent a lot of time together. We sure were lucky to have such good friends.

North to Hayward Again

We took another trip up to Hayward to see Grandma. We were able to take Dan with us on this trip. Bryan couldn't come along as he was only going to be 2 years old. He still liked to stay at home with his Mom and Dad. While we were in Hayward I watched Dan go fishing. I was hoping he would catch one, but no luck. He went fishing a couple of times.

Mom kept trying to get me to go swimming but I wasn't too impressed with that. I would much rather just walk up to the bottom of my chest and enjoy the water from there. Mom wanted to make sure I could swim so she took me out into deeper water. Of course I could swim! -- all dogs can, but I headed back to shore quickly. Mom said she was happy as they had a neighbor once that had a dog that couldn't swim, he would sink straight to the bottom and just walk around. His owner had to go down and get him. I guess knowing that, it made Mom feel better; but it just made me really wet. Mom said I looked like a drowned rat when I got all wet, which did not make me feel that much better about it, to be honest. My beautiful long hair took a while to dry so I rolled in the grass to help it dry faster.

That wasn't my only taste of swimming. I loved to chase Dan around the yard. We would run and run and it would make me tired so I would sleep well at night. One time when I was chasing Dan, he ran out on the dock with me in close pursuit. Well, I didn't know he was going to stop! I was running alongside him by then and in I went with a big splash! I was not ready for that and I was a little scared (actually a lot scared). I swam to the dock and tried to climb up, but I couldn't. Mom had been close by and she jumped in and aimed me to the shore. I did not enjoy that and have learned a lesson. I bet they won't be able to do that to me again.

I was just starting to figure out how life goes and how a year works. It seems that we do pretty much the same kinds of things each year. I figured I liked the way we did things and looked forward to the rest of the year; with the holidays and all the good food. Little did I know what was going to happen in the near future that would change my mind about this.

Cindy Leaves

My first real shocker was the day that I heard that my sister was leaving. She told me she was going to go to work on a cruise ship and she would be gone from home for long periods of time. I didn't want her to go. I love it when she calls me "Jake-a-rooni." She did explain to me that she had worked on cruise ships before I was born and she really liked it. She said she was going to be doing something different this time, she was going to be a shopping guide. She would help the women find places to shop in the different ports. This seemed pretty strange to me, I didn't think women needed help in finding places to shop! (Dad told me this.)

Let me tell you, the first few weeks that Cindy was gone I was pretty sad. I really missed her and all the attention she gave me. She would always sit on the floor by me and scratch me. I would let her do this as long as she wanted.

Even though I missed her, life was still good, especially with Dan and Bryan always coming over and willing to share a snack with me. Then there was our daily walk which we do every day. There was still all of the fun when we got together with Bev and Dale and Dave and Sue. We still had a lot of good times. I just had this little void in my heart not having Cindy, but I knew she loved me and I understood she had to work for a living. She called almost every week and she would talk to me. I would know it was her when I heard her favorite saying: "Jake-a-rooni dog." Boy, it sure made a young dog happy to hear that.

Fall and Winter

Dad told me that now that I was over one year old there was something very, very important for me to learn about. He said he hadn't bothered me with it when I was younger, as I wouldn't have understood. He said that I needed to become a Green Bay Packer Fan. I knew Mom and Dad went to a lot of Milwaukee Brewer games but I didn't know about the Packers. He said they watch them on TV every week. He said this was the year they could maybe go to the Super Bowl. Knowing that I wore bandanas pretty well, Mom made me one for the Packers. I would wear it on game days. I heard some pretty funny things. Dad and Dave got together each week for football games. They would alternate where they watched them. They said that each week they had to cook a fro-

zen pizza at half time. They said they also couldn't wear anything that had Packers on them. They said I was the only one allowed to wear anything that had to do with the Packers. I asked Dad why Dale didn't join him and Dave at the games. He told me that Dale liked to watch the game all by himself and not have anyone around. This all had something to do with their superstitions about the game. Wow, and I thought they were adults! I hear football does that to a guy! Whatever they did seemed to work as the Packers kept winning and winning.

Mom was really getting into making me these bandanas. Next she made me one for Halloween. She said if the kids all dressed up, then I should have been dressed up too. The kids that came to the door got candy and I just got to look at how funny they looked all dressed up. Some of the kids I recognized were neighborhood kids. They sure seemed to enjoy this Trick or Treating thing. I knew Mom and Dad enjoyed it too. Mom was crazy about Halloween like Dad was about football, because she had the whole house decorated and she even put on Halloween clothes for Trick or Treat.

Meanwhile, the Green Bay Packers were still winning. They were in first place in their division. Everyone was going Super Bowl crazy in our state. As fall continued, I knew what was coming...my two favorite holidays: Thanksgiving and Christmas. I still helped Mom in the kitchen at Thanksgiving and cleaned up anything that fell on the floor, plus whatever I could beg for. It almost drove me nuts. The house smelled so good. I did get to sample some of the smells, so I was really happy. Then, when Mom cleaned the meat off the bones after dinner, I was right there with her again...*yum!*

Next came another wonderful time of the year, when Mom made *COOKIES!* You know, that was my favorite word. *Wow!* Once again she was making so many cookies, why it would have taken even me a long time to eat all of them and then I would have probably gotten a stomach ache. Mom was nice and gave me a taste of cookie dough every once in a while. She talked to Dad and told him which were her favorites and he told her which were his. My favorites were easy....*ALL* of them!

Christmas

Once again our house had changed completely. It was all decorated for Christmas. Mom said Christmas was her favorite holiday. Why, we even had Christmas dishes. I guess I was too small to notice that last year. The house looked really pretty. Again they had brought a Christmas tree into the house and had it all decorated.

On Christmas Day the house was full of people again and everyone was snacking on cookies and other goodies. They really had a good time. I made sure that I stayed close to my little buddy Bryan as I knew I could always get food from him. I just needed to be careful, as one time Bryan set a cookie on the edge of the coffee table and I ate it. Mom yelled at me that I shouldn't take food off the table. I knew I shouldn't, but it was just *sooooo* tempting. Christmas was really a lot of fun. The only thing that would have made it better was if Cindy could have been there with us. She still called every week.

I almost forgot, everyone in Wisconsin was still going crazy as the Packers were in the playoffs. They said it had been a long time since they had been there. They sure yelled a lot when they watched the games on TV. I could tell the difference between good and bad, when they would stand up and yell *"YES,"* that was good; but when they yelled *"NO"* (or other words I won't repeat here) that was bad. I enjoyed just watching them. When they would yell *"YES"* a lot, I would get up and bark so they would think I was watching with them.

A Year That Would Have Many Changes

Winter and Football

Let's talk football. I thought that everyone had been football crazy during the regular season, but that was nothing compared to the playoffs. Each week was really something else...it got crazier and crazier with each game that the Packers won. I thought everyone was celebrating every day, they were wearing Packer clothes and hats every single day. Not only that, but the main topic of any conversation always ended up being the Packers.

Well, it happened! The Packers won the Super Bowl!! Mom and Dad were over at Dave and Sue's across the street. I knew they were excited because with my good hearing, I could hear them yelling from our house. I was home alone and knew they were yelling *"YES"* a lot, so I just got up and barked anyway. I wanted to be a Packers Fan too.

Scott and Linda came to visit us at our house and they brought Brewer along. I was telling Brewer how crazy these people were about football and how the Packers won the Super Bowl. They were still wearing a lot of Packers clothes. Scott and Dad even made Brewer a Packers cap. You know, I went along with the Packers scarf but I drew the line when it came to the hat thing. Have you ever seen those cheese head hats?

I Went to Spring Training (Sort of)

Mom and Dad said that we were going to make a trip to Florida. There were three reasons for this trip. First, we were going to see Uncle Bill and Aunt Kathy. Second, there was Spring Training in Florida. The third reason I wasn't too crazy about. Dad said that he needed to find a new job and that we may be moving out of Wisconsin. He was going on a job interview in Atlanta. *Wow!* I hated to think of moving away from all our friends.

Well, it was off to Florida we went. I knew that I was a good car rider but I had never been in the car for so long at one time. We drove and drove and drove. We would stop for gas and some food and to let me out, but we were in the car all day long. Dad said that we would be staying overnight in Georgia. Then, in the morning we would be able to get up early and get to Uncle Bill's at a good time.

We spent the night in a place called a motel. I never knew they had such places. It was just a small room with a bed, a dresser and a TV. Oh yes, and a bathroom. I was just thinking that I wouldn't want to live there, not much space. I must admit I was a little frightened but also protective. I would hear people walking outside our room and I would bark. I wasn't too sure of myself, so I kind of barked with a question mark sound. Mom told me it was okay, And to just go to sleep because we had to get up and start driving early in the morning.

The next morning we were off again. We got to Uncle Bill's early in the afternoon. I was glad to see my cousin Sean again and I ran right up to him. I also liked seeing Uncle Bill and Aunt Kathy. Uncle Bill was holding his dog. He was small and his name was Bandit. Dad told me he was a Jack Russell Terrier. Once I got to know him we had a lot of fun together. He was full grown but I was a lot bigger than him. Later, some other people came over that I found out were cousins. Man, I didn't know we had so many relatives, but I sure had fun with all the kids.

One day Mom and Dad took me to watch some spring baseball. I had to stay on my leash but that was okay because I wouldn't want to get lost— I didn't know where we were. It would be a long walk home to Wisconsin. I kind of enjoyed watching the baseball players practicing. Mom and Dad knew one of them and got a chance to talk to him.

On the way back to Uncle Bill's we stopped where there was a bunch of water. We got out and Mom walked me

into the water. After I got in a ways, I figured I would get a quick drink like I did at Grandma's, but …*pugh*!!!!! It tasted terrible. I shook my head and tried to get the taste out of my mouth. Mom said that was salt water from the Gulf of Mexico. I know one thing, I don't ever want to go back in that stuff. Mom took me back to the car and gave me some good water to drink. It took a lot to get that salty taste out of my mouth.

After almost a week Dad said it was time to head back home. We drove from Tampa to Atlanta, Georgia where we stayed in one of those motel things again. I still think I like houses better. The next day, Dad went on a job interview. When he was finished with that we got back in the car for another long drive. We stopped overnight in Indianapolis and spent the night with Scott, Linda and Brewer. The next morning we headed home. It was a fun vacation but it was nice to get back home and be able to curl up in my own bean bag chair again.

Our Upcoming Move

Dad made himself an office out of Cindy's room. He would work on his computer and call and talk to people about getting a new job. Every once in a while he would be gone for a few days and I was told he was out on a job interview. I would be really happy to see him each time he got home.

Seemed with all the activity, the time went by pretty fast. One good thing happened, Cindy came home. She said she would be home for a couple of months and then she had to go back out to sea on the cruise ship. With everything going on I sure was happy to see her. Mom and Dad seemed a little stressed out about possibly moving.

Then I got the word that yes, we indeed would be moving. Dad got a job in Alabama, so we would be moving there. I had no idea what was ahead and again I was a little hesitant. I'm almost 2 years old, but I am still Mom and Dad's little boy.

The next thing you know, there was a big going away party for us. All of our friends and family from the area came. Dad would be the first one to leave while Mom and I would stay home and work on selling the house. I remember the morning that Dad left. Kevin and the boys were there along with Cindy, Bev and Dale, and Dave and Sue. I noticed that Dad started to cry as he was saying goodbye and he told Mom that he had to leave. I'm glad I got my hug in. Mom went out to the car with Dad and when she came back in she was crying.I know one thing, I didn't like things like this to happen but Mom explained it's all a part of life and we would be okay.

It wasn't long and Mom seemed pretty happy. She told Cindy and me that we sold our house. She couldn't believe that the first people that came through it were the ones that bought it. I knew that even though she was happy, she was also sad about having to leave everyone in Wisconsin.

I was really happy when Dad came home for my 2nd Birthday. Since the house had sold so fast, he came home to help Mom get some of the items ready to move. We did still celebrate my birthday, but I could tell that Mom and Dad had a lot on their minds. I realized that my role in this family was about to become much more important. I knew they were going to need me to hug them and help them feel more comfortable when we finally moved. Even though I am young, I will be up to the task and do whatever I can to make Mom and Dad happy. I wonder if this could be the reason that I was born, to help Mom and Dad through this tough time.

Dad was only home for a few days with us, but one day he cuddled up to me on the floor. He told me how lonesome he would get in Alabama. He said coming home to an empty house wasn't for him. He liked it much better when he had me and Mom to be with him. He said he would be happy when we were all together again in Alabama.

After Dad went back to Alabama it wasn't long and the movers came and took all our furniture. Then it was off to Alabama for us too. Poor Cindy, she was only home for the summer and we had to put her through all this. She left a day before Mom and I did and headed to Alabama. When Mom and I left, we stopped for the night at Scott and Linda's house in Indianapolis. The next morning it was back in the car and heading to our new home.

I will never forget this day—July 15th. We arrived in Birmingham in the middle of the afternoon after having a lot of road construction just north of Birmingham. All I knew was Mom wanted to get out of the traffic and get to our new house. Dad had given us directions and a key to get in if we should get there before he got home from work. *Wow!* It was really *HOT* when we got out of the car. Mom said it was like 95 degrees. We had started to take some of the things into our new house when Dad arrived.

This new house was really small, it was kind of like one of those motels we had stayed at, only it had a little living room and a small kitchen. Dad told me not to worry, this wasn't going to be our house, it was just a little apartment he rented until we were able to sell the house. It was just nice to have us all together again in one place. I could see that Dad was really happy to have us. I remembered how he had told me how home sick he would get once in a while. I could tell that Mom missed him too when they would talk on the phone. I was just really happy that we were all together again. I started to rev up my loving as I knew Mom and Dad really needed me to be close to them during this time.

Our New Rental Home

We were only in the little apartment that Dad stayed in for about a week. Mom and Dad said they had found a house for us to rent. (They told me that we would stay there until they either found a house to buy or build.)

I sure was happy when I saw the movers bringing in our own furniture. Now I knew we were together again as a family. I also knew that I was going to have to step up and make Mom and Dad happy in Alabama. I also knew Cindy would be going back on the ship, so then it would be just me with Mom and Dad. It seemed like it was way too soon for Cindy to go back to work, but the time came and just me, Mom, and Dad were left in our little house. This house is pretty small because Mom and Dad had to put a lot of boxes in the basement without even opening them. They said they would stay there until we moved again.

There was one thing in our new house that was really neat. It had windows that were really low. Not only could I see out of them standing up, but I could lay down and rest my head on the window sill. That was really neat. I could spend a lot of time watching what was going on outside.

Even though it was really hot outside, we still went for our daily walks. Only thing missing was Mom not being able to drag Dave along as he was a long way away in Wisconsin. Dad still took plastic bags along and when I did a job he picked it up. He said it was important for people with pets to make sure they cleaned up after them.

Our backyard was pretty big and had a fence almost all the

 way around it. Dad finished it by adding a little fence on each side of the house. Now I was free to romp in the yard as they knew I couldn't run away. The people next door had two dogs and we would run up and down along the fence line. We got a lot of exercise doing this.

I found something in my yard that I really didn't like; fire ants. I stepped into a pile of them and I started yelping. Mom came to my rescue and cleaned them all off of me and washed my feet in cold water. I knew that won't happen to me again! I wondered how the bites of such little things could hurt so bad. I guessed I would have to put these little critters on my list of things I didn't like.

Christmas in Alabama

With our first Christmas coming, Mom and Dad decorated the house. They didn't do as much as they did in Wisconsin but they said they would do more when we built a house. I know I've told you about car rides but now Mom and I really did some driving. We drove all the way from Birmingham to northern Wisconsin to get Grandma. We stopped in Indianapolis each way to spend the night. With this long trip, I sure was glad that Mom liked to snack so much while driving. She was really good at sharing with me. I would go from the back seat to the front seat with her. It was nice in the front as I could see where we were going–but most importantly, I was close to the goodies.

When we got to Hayward, I found out that Buttons had died. I wondered if he went to the "Rainbow Bridge." Mom explained that her Dad had died when Buttons was a young dog. She said that she was sure that her Dad (Grandpa I never met) was there to greet her when she got there. It would be straight into Heaven for Buttons with Grandpa. We got Grandma's things together and then back in the car we went, headed back home to Birmingham with an overnight stop in Indianapolis. The next day when we got home I thought that I had had enough car riding for a while. I liked riding but *Wow!* that was a lot. Besides, if I rode that much all the time, I might get fat eating all the *yum, yum* goodies.

It was nice to have Grandma with us at Christmas. It was really different this year, we didn't have a house full of people. I knew Mom and Dad missed this so I cuddled up to them a little more and gave them "extra" doggie charm. It wasn't too long however before we had some more company. Dad's cousin Eddie and Mindy that I had met several times at our house in Wisconsin came by for a few days. They said they went to Florida for a month each Winter. They were there in time for us to all watch the Packers in the Super Bowl again. The results weren't so good this time, they lost to Denver. With Christmas and football I realized something very different. It was cold and snowy in Wisconsin when we went to get Grandma but in Alabama it was really nice. Mom explained to me about how the weather was different and we wouldn't have real cold weather and almost no snow. I know Mom likes snow, so I wondered how this would sit with her.

With Cindy back on a ship, Mom and Dad took Grandma to Florida to see her aboard the ship while she was in port. Mom said I couldn't go along and our neighbors were going to watch me. They said I could stay in the house and they would come and feed me and let me out. After that long ride to Wisconsin and back, I was content to stay home. They went to Tampa on the way home and spent a day with Uncle Bill, Aunt Kathy, and Sean.

It wasn't long after that and it was time to take Grandma home. She was with us for over a month but it sure didn't seem that long. Once again, Mom and I did our road trip marathon. Yup, I was right, Mom does miss the snow. When we got to Grandma's house Mom was really excited to see snow again. I guess living in Alabama, she will have to travel in the winter to see snow. Mom liked having me to talk to on the way home after we dropped Grandma off. I liked having her to share her goodies with me.

Mom and Dad did a lot of looking at houses and then finally told me they were going to build a house. They told me it would be a lot bigger than our little rental house. Even though we had a small house while we built, we got a lot of company from Wisconsin. In addition to Eddie and Mindy, we were also visited by Dave and Sue, with Lynnice and Ian.

Then, Scott and Linda came and visited also. I could see how happy it made Mom and Dad to get company. I think they were pretty lonesome after moving from Wisconsin. I am, however, still doing that "little extra" to make their days special.

Getting Settled in Alabama

Our New House

We went to our new house a lot. I got to learn something new. I had never seen a house being built before. There were a few times that it was pretty scary. I was a little afraid to go up some of the stairs as you could see all the way down into the base-ment. Mom told me not to be afraid, when the house was finished, you wouldn't be able to see this.

It wasn't long and the house was finished and it was time for us to move in. Dad rented a truck and our neighbors helped us move. They started to move on Friday night and after loading the truck it started to rain. When I got to the house with Mom in the car, I went straight inside and stayed there. Dad backed the truck in the driveway so he could get close to the house to keep from getting too wet. Most of the first load was boxes Mom had packed in Ala-bama, plus the boxes she never opened at our rental house. While they were unloading, I did my own exploring. I liked the main floor, it had the kitchen and family room and Mom and Dad's bedroom. Man, you should see how big their bathroom was, it was probably bigger than the entire bedroom at the rental house. Oh, and the windows were low just like in the rental. I could lay on the floor and put my head on the sill and check out everything that went on outside.

Speaking of outside, our new house had a lot of trees in the back-yard. I had noticed that there were a lot of squirrels running around. Of course I barked at them from inside the house but that didn't scare them one bit. Whenever Mom or

Dad let me out, I would make a beeline for the backyard and look for those squirrels. We only had grass in the front yard, so when I would run around in the backyard, I got pretty dusty and Mom had to clean me off before I could go back into the house.

Our first visitors to stay with us at our new house were Scott and Linda. It was really nice to have company in our new house. Scott had a customer of his that lived in Birmingham so he also included going to see him while he was in town.

New Walking Areas

We had a really neat place to walk near our new house. There was a park only about three blocks away. Mom and Dad would walk me on my leash until we got to the park and then they would let me run free. Man, you wouldn't believe how much fun that was. I could run into all of the woods and chase all kinds of critters. I guess Mom and Dad didn't realize how fast I could run until they saw me in the park. We would be walking and all of a sudden, I would see a squirrel way ahead of us. Let me tell you, I would take off like a jet and run after it. I would hear Mom and Dad talking that they didn't even see the squirrel. After running around, I would be ready for a rest when we got home. Another nice thing about our house was that the air conditioning vents are on the floor. *Wow!* I could lay right there on the vent and cool off, while still watching everything outside the window.

Walking in the park was only the beginning. We found a couple of really neat places to walk. One was in the park where Mom and Dad usually walked on the roadway. There was a trail they could walk on that would wind through the woods. I really liked walking there because there were a million things I could smell and a lot of critters to chase. It was a pretty good walk for Mom and Dad and plenty of exercise for me with all the running I did back and forth. The other place was also really cool, there was a dirt road that led to another trail and that trail led to the very top of a big hill. It got pretty steep near the top so I would have to wait for Mom and Dad a couple of times to catch up with me. At the top the view was really neat, you could see a long way and there were a lot of rocks for me to climb on. Mom said the view from up there reminded her of the Smoky Mountains, but on a smaller scale. I was never there, so I didn't really know what the Smoky Mountains were like, but they must have been pretty spectacular because if these were a small-scale version of them, I couldn't imagine how neat they would be. We used to make that trip up the big hill every Sunday morning as our exercise walk. I would have bet our walking partners from Wisconsin, Dave and Sue would have really liked this. I knew Mom said they would take them up there when they came to visit. One thing Mom and Dad would do to me was try and fool me. After walking on these trails a few times, I got to know where we were going and would run ahead. Then Mom and Dad would call me and they would start to walk another way. I would have to run really fast to come back to them and then onto the new path. Well, what they were doing was just kidding me, they were actually going the original way but they said this gave me a lot of extra exercise. I fell for this a few times but I learned real quick and started just stopping when then called and said they were going another way because I knew they were probably just kidding me. I was usually right! Remember me telling you how smart I am?

I also found out something that I liked while walking in the woods. I could go into the woods and go potty and have complete privacy. I liked not having anyone see me go potty. I knew Dad cleaned up after me so we didn't leave a mess in anyone's yard but I really liked going into the woods and being all by myself.

Our First Vacation

We hadn't been in our house too long when it came time to take a vacation trip to Wisconsin. Of course you know by now that I don't mind those car trips, especially with all the goodies Mom takes along. The only difference was that with Dad along, I had to stay in the back seat for the entire trip. It was okay though because Dad made me a little bed that I could lay on and be almost right between them. Did I mention how close I was to the goodies with this spot? *Yum!*

When we got to Wisconsin we stayed with Dave and Sue because my brother Kevin lived in a small apartment. It was pretty neat at Dave and Sue's. They had a rec room in the basement and their couch opened up to a bed. It was really nice, but I was just glad to be with Mom and Dad and seeing what a good time they were having visiting everyone.

It was so nice to see everyone again. Seems like there were parties going on all the time. They had a lot of cook-outs so guess who I stayed near? You got it, by Bryan because I remembered how he would always share his food with me. We really had a good time, and we got to see everyone who we used to see and have over when we lived in Wisconsin. I know Mom and Dad really liked being around all their friends again. I almost forgot how much they like a lot of people around. They really seemed to be soaking up all of these get-togethers.

The only strange part of the vacation was looking across the street to where we used to live and knowing that some other people lived there now. It sure did bring back some good memories for me. I'm pretty sure Mom and Dad missed not living there and being able to visit all these people on a more regular basis.

A More Normal Life

Well, once we were back in Alabama things had really settled down nicely and our new house was really starting to feel like home. Mom had it set up the way she wanted it. We even put in grass in the backyard. Mom planted a lot of bushes on one side of the house where there was a hill. She said that way she wouldn't have to cut the grass on a steep hill. The other side of the house had the driveway so I figured she was pretty smart in doing this.

After the grass in the back was nice and strong, I was able to run around and not get all dusty. Mom and Dad started a new game, they would pretend to chase me and I would run around. I would run all the way around the house. Remember how I told you I surprised them by my speed in running? Well, they gave me a nickname when we would do this; they called me "Jet Dog." I thought this was pretty cool and besides I did run like a jet.

I'm sure you also remember me telling you how smart I am. Well, here is another example of my smart thinking. When we would play jet dog in the yard, I would run around and around

and guess what? I would get dizzy after a while and have to lie down as everything was spinning around. Then I tried something. When I ran around in the backyard, I tried running in a figure 8. That way I would change directions and not get so dizzy. I could run a lot without having to take a break. Of course when I did finish with this game, it was kind of nice to just lie in the cool grass and roll around in it. I sure am glad they put this yard in.

While we were on vacation in Wisconsin, Dad's third cousin Lindsay said she wanted to make a trip to Alabama in August. I can remember Mom telling her that she really wouldn't like coming to Alabama in August because it was too hot. Well, that didn't do any good so in August, here comes Lindsay and her Mom Bev, Dad's second cousin (man-o-man this relative thing is hard to keep up with, even for a smart dog like me). Anyway, after they came to Alabama, Lindsay realized why Mom tried to talk her out of coming in August. It was always hot in Alabama in the summer but August was the hottest. We did have fun and were able to sit out on the deck at night after it cooled off a little.

The Years Roll On

Christmas in Wisconsin

Another road trip in the winter for a trip north to Wisconsin. Grandma wasn't going to come to Alabama so Mom and Dad decided to go north for the holidays. Once again, we stayed at Dave and Sue's and once again we had a lot of parties going on. We also got a chance to see all of our old friends. With the colder weather we couldn't party outside so everything was inside. Plus, we went visiting other people's houses. We were at Bev and Dale's and also at Kevin's house. Oh, and another neat thing was that my sister Cindy was able to come to Wisconsin too. I can tell you that her and Dad were not all that crazy about the cold weather and the snow. Mom sure liked it though and she even got a chance to shovel a couple of times.

We left Wisconsin so that we could stop in Indianapolis and spend New Years with Scott and Linda. Would you believe the day we got there, we got a lot of snow? I thought Mom was going to stay outside all day shoveling. After a fun time with Scott and Linda we had to head home to

Alabama so Dad could go back to work.

Spring Trips

The next spring, Mom and Dad made a couple of trips. The first was a long weekend where they met Dad's brother Uncle Doug and Aunt Bev, his wife. They also met up with Eddie and Mindy and celebrated Mardi Gras in New Orleans, whatever that means. Their second trip started out okay as Dave and Sue came to visit for a few days. We took them on a walk up the mountain where I said they would like to go. I had lots of fun with Lynnice and Ian. We climbed on all the rocks.

After a few days, I had to go to the vet's house to stay. Mom and Dad couldn't get anyone to take care of me while they went to the beach with Dave and Sue. I'm sure they had a good time, but it sure was a long week for me waiting for them to come home. When I saw Mom in the office when she came to get me, I was so excited that I piddled on the floor—and that's not like me. I am trained very well and am very smart, it's just that I was so happy I could not control myself.

Summing Up My Story

You know, I could go on and on about my life, but I'm sure by now you have a pretty good idea. I had a great life and I know that I helped make Mom and Dad's life a little brighter. I also must say that I am truly grateful that I was the dog they picked to live with them.

Before I came along, Mom and Dad had said they wouldn't have another dog. I believe that a higher power led them to get another dog and I was the chosen one. I helped them overcome some very hard times with missing family in Wisconsin. They in turn treated me just like a family member and not a dog.

I have some other funny things to tell you about but first I must tell you about me going to the Rainbow Bridge. I was 12 years old and I got cancer. I had one operation but it came back so I had to leave and go to the Rainbow Bridge. Don't feel sorry for me as I am really happy here. I am so thankful to Mom and Dad and my sister Cindy for all the love they gave me. I will continue to watch over them until the day comes that they come and join me and we are together again.

There are a lot of neat things here, but I especially like being able to meet Mom and Dad's previous dogs; Samantha, Cha-Sam, and Rusty. Boy, you should see Cha-Sam catch the Frisbee. I don't think she ever misses it, and *wow*, can she jump! I sit with Rusty and we just watch her. I have shown Cha-Sam my game of chasing shadows and guess what, I am better at this than she is. I must admit though, she is better at the Frisbee, I still don't like that game.

Rusty was cross-eyed when he was alive and in fact lost the vision in one eye while on earth. Well, he is fine now. He used to have problems catching the Frisbee because of his eyesight but he does okay now whenever Cha-Sam lets him play.

From here I would like to tell you about some of the other things that happened. These are still good memories to me and I'm sure Mom and Dad will always remember them also.

Memories

In this chapter I will tell you some of my memories. Some of them are pretty funny now that I look back on them. They were all a part of a wonderful life. I wish every dog could have the life that I had.

Stare Down Contest

Dad used to have fun with this. Once in a while I would be sitting down and Dad would look at me. When I looked at him he would just stare at me and I would know I hadn't done anything wrong. He would just stare at me. I would look away and then look back and see him still staring at me. I would keep looking away and then back. After a while I would cry a little and he would call me over and hug me and scratch my ears. I always knew what he was doing, but I never could beat him at this game. I did however like the extra attention he gave me after he won.

Talking at the Bottom of the Stairs

This was another thing I did with Dad a lot. With our house being built on a hill, our garage was in the basement. When Dad would come home I would always run downstairs and meet him. He would sit on a step and love on me.

I would be so excited I would start to cry and then he would talk to me kind of like a growl and I would growl back. Then he would get louder and so would I. This would go on for a while and usually stop when Mom yelled down for us to "knock it off." If Mom would happen to be on the phone when Dad came home, she would stop us really quickly or she couldn't hear the person she was talking to. Dad and I really liked to play this game.

Cookie Time

I know I've told you several times in my story how smart I am. Well, let me give you another example. Each night Mom would get me a cookie at about 7 p.m. If the time came and she didn't get my cookie, I would stand between the dining area and the family room and cry a little to get their attention. Sure enough, Mom or Dad would get up and get me my cookie.

Another cookie time was when I went outside before bedtime. When I came in, I always got a cookie. Dad would sometimes try to fool me and not give me a cookie. I would cry and he would ignore me so I would come right up to him. Sometimes he would then walk around the house and I would follow until I got my cookie. When he did this, I would also get some of that extra loving from Dad and once in a while an extra cookie.

Spelling

As you are probably aware, most dogs understand a lot of words. Well, you can include me in that group. But then, I can also understand spelling. Mom or Dad would want to tell the other something without my knowing so they would try and spell it to each other. They couldn't fool me as I know these words when they spell them out: c-o-o-k-i-e, w-a-l-k, c-a-r, n-a-p, o-u-t-s-i-d-e.

Bed Time

Each night when I knew it was bedtime, I would go by the bedroom door and look back at Mom and Dad. If they didn't come I would cry a little. Then, if they were going to stay up a while they would tell me to "go to bed" and I'd turn around and get in my big comfortable bean bag bed.

Mom and Dad's bed is the only piece of furniture I would get on. Even then, I would only get on it if I was invited up on the bed by one of them. At bedtime, they would always call me up and I would only stay for a few minutes as my bed, or the floor, was much more to my liking.

There were a few times that I would stay on the bed. Each day, Mom would take a nap and she would call me up. With Dad being at work, there was much more room for me so I would stay on the bed. As a matter of fact, sometimes when Mom got up, I stayed in bed for a while myself. (Mom takes too short a nap for me.) Another time I would stay in bed was on the weekend. When I knew it was about time to get up, I would go to Mom's side of the bed and cry. She would wake up and then get up. I knew it was the weekend so I would then jump up in bed with Dad and take a nap with him until he got up.

Every night I would sleep either in Mom and Dad's bedroom or on the floor in the bathroom as the tile floor was nice and cool. The only time I changed from this was when Cindy was home or when we had company. I would start out in Mom and Dad's room but after they were asleep, I would go out to the family room near the stairs. That way I could be on the watch for anyone upstairs. After all, I am a dog and have to take care of everyone when they are sleeping. Dad knew that I did this because he usually got up during the night and knew I was there.

Burping

Now this may seem strange to you but I was always a dog that burped. You know how most dogs pass gas and it smells? Well, not with me. I never had gas (at least any that smelled) but I did burp. Mom and Dad would always laugh when I burped but then they knew that was better than passing gas. You wouldn't believe how loud I could burp once in a while. I think I could even beat Dad in a burping contest.

Thunderstorms

When I was younger, I was never afraid of thunderstorms. I just ignored them. Mom told me how some of their other dogs would be afraid and huff and puff during a storm. Then one day this changed. We had a really bad thunderstorm and a bolt of lightning struck a tree one house away. Man, you wouldn't believe how loud it was. I really didn't like that. From that day on, I didn't like thunderstorms. I didn't huff and puff, but I did go and hide. Dad had a neat closet that you went into and then around a corner. It was nice and quiet and dark. I would just go in there and curl up in the corner. Once Mom and Dad knew this, they always kept a pair of Dads pants on the floor–that helped make me feel better.

You know how dogs have such good hearing don't you? Well, I could always tell Mom and Dad a storm was coming because as soon as I heard the slightest rumble of thunder, off I went into Dad's closet. I liked this hiding area so well, that when I would be left alone at home, a lot of times, I would go into the closet. This was my safe place.

Shopping with Mom

When it wasn't too warm outside (which isn't often in Alabama) Mom would take me shopping with her. When she went into the store I would sit in the driver's seat and watch for her. I wasn't exactly crazy about being alone as I really don't like strangers. When someone would come by and look at me or talk to me I would just look straight ahead and pretend they weren't there. I never barked at people like some of the other dogs I see in parking lots. A couple of times Mom was coming out when someone was trying to talk to me. They told Mom it was really funny how I just ignored them when they came by. I was just glad that Mom locked the doors when she left me as I don't know what I would do if a stranger opened the door.

How this Book Started

This book came about because while Cindy was out to sea on a cruise ship, I would write her an email. Mom told Dad he should save the emails and write a book. Well, the emails are lost but now there is the book.

I can remember some of the funny things from these emails. I had a hard time at first because I misspelled words. I knew how to spell, but my paws were too big for the keyboard. Do you have any idea how hard it is for a dog to hit only one key at a time? It's not easy and it took a lot of practice but I got the hang of it. Then I found out about the very special item that computers have, it's called "spell check." Wow! Does that ever work neat? I felt like I became a genius overnight.

Once in a while I would send her a picture of me. I could never figure out how Dad set the camera so that he could rush around and get in the picture. Well, I snuck out Dad's camera and I tried and tried and I always came up with a blank picture. I couldn't get around fast enough. At first I thought, *WOW*, Dad sure is fast but after *MANY* tries, I discovered the little button on the camera that would let me get around and into the picture. Cindy really liked it when I sent a picture with my emails.

Oh wait! I have just a few more things to tell you and show you in one more chapter.

About the Photos In
This Book

You know how I've mentioned how many pictures my Dad took of me, well let me explain something. When I was first adopted, my Dad had an old fashioned film camera. He had to buy film and then after taking pictures he would have to take them to a store and they would develop them. This of course cost money. Later on in my life, Dad bought a digital camera and he could take as many pictures as he wanted and he could do his own developing on his computer. I would just like to add a few more pictures here to show you what good pictures I take.

These first 3 pictures I am *VERY* proud of. I was so lucky to have my Birthday on July 4th which is the celebration of our country's independence. Get me a flag and I am ready for you to take my picture.

Okay, remember how I said I hate to get my beautiful hair wet? Well, here's why. I have to roll around in the grass a lot to dry off.

Here's a few more of my holiday dress-ups:

Here is a picture with Cindy, the very special sister that gave me the nickname "Jake-a-Rooni."

Then my two favorite little guys that I loved to play with (and get snacks from) Dan and Bryan.

Next is a very special picture for a couple of reasons. First it has Mom, Dad, Cindy, Dan and Bryan all together. The other reason is that Dad is in the picture. Usually he is always on the other side of the camera.

Here is one of me laying on the deck in Birmingham with the temperature showing 120 degrees. After a while I would have to

go in the house and lay over the air conditioning vent to cool off.

And to finish off, some of my favorite pictures of *ME!*

With that I guess it's time to end this story. I had a wonderful life and hope that everyone has an opportunity to share a *TWO-* way love with a dog. We will give you so much love you won't know what to do with it. And remember if and when you get a dog: The dog may not be your entire life but you will be their entire life.

~ The End ~

Printed by Amazon Italia Logistica S.r.l.
Torrazza Piemonte (TO), Italy

28271590R00058